A
GOLDEN TREASURY
— OF —
NURSERY VERSE

A
GOLDEN TREASURY
— OF —
NURSERY VERSE

COMPILED BY MARK DANIEL

PAVILION
MICHAEL JOSEPH

For Pauline

Conceived and produced by
Breslich & Foss
Golden House
28-31 Great Pulteney Street
London W1R 3DD

Design: Roger Daniels
Editor: Ailsa Heritage

First published in Great Britain in 1986 by
Pavilion Books Limited
196 Shaftesbury Avenue, London WC2H 8JL
in association with Michael Joseph Limited
27 Wrights Lane, Kensington, London W8 5DZ

British Library Cataloguing in Publication Data
A golden treasury of nursery verse
1. Children's poetry, English
I. Daniel, Mark, *1954–*
821'.8'0809282   PR1195.C47

ISBN 1 85145 086 6

Photoset in Great Britain by Lineage Limited
Originated by Dot Gradations Limited
Printed and bound in Italy by Arnoldo Mondadori

All colour pictures are courtesy of
Fine Art Photographic Library, London

CONTENTS

DAYBREAK
~ 7 ~

THE CLASSROOM
~ 23 ~

PLAYTIME
~ 41 ~

SUNNY DAYS
~ 57 ~

ALL CREATURES
GREAT AND SMALL
~ 79 ~

SOME OLD FRIENDS
~ 109 ~

SWEET DREAMS
~ 125 ~

THE POETS
~ 148 ~

THE PAINTERS
~ 151 ~

INDEX OF FIRST LINES
~ 152 ~

DAYBREAK

TIME TO RISE

A birdie with a yellow bill
Hopped upon the window sill,
Cocked his shining eye and said:
'Ain't you 'shamed, you sleepy-head?

ROBERT LOUIS STEVENSON

A Child's Garden of Verses, 1885

Cocks crow in the morn
To tell us to rise,
And he who lies late
Will never be wise;
For early to bed
And early to rise
Makes a man healthy
And wealthy and wise.

ANON

SLUG-ABED

Get up, get up, you lazyhead,
Get up, you lazy sinner!
We need those sheets for tablecloths –
It's nearly time for dinner!

ANON

Donkey, donkey, old and gray,
Ope your mouth, and gently bray;
Lift your ears and blow your horn,
To wake the world this sleepy morn.

ANON

Cock Robin got up early
At the break of day,
And went to Jenny's window
To sing a roundelay,
He sang Cock Robin's love
To the little Jenny Wren,
And when he got unto the end,
Then he began again.

ANON

THE WIND

Who has seen the wind?
   Neither I nor you;
But when the leaves hang trembling
   The wind is passing through.

Who has seen the wind?
   Neither you nor I;
But when the trees bow down their heads
   The wind is passing by.

CHRISTINA GEORGINA ROSSETTI

Sing-Song, 1872

THE THROSTLE

"Summer is coming, summer is coming,
I know it, I know it, I know it.
Light again, leaf again, love again,"
Yes, my wild little poet.

Sing the new year in under the blue,
Last year you sang it as gladly,
"New, new, new, new!" Is it then *so* new
That you should carol so madly?

"Love again, song again, nest again, young again,"
Never a prophet so crazy!
And hardly a daisy as yet, little friend,
See, there is hardly a daisy.

"Here again, here, here, here, happy year!"
O, warble unchidden, unbidden!
Summer is coming, is coming, my dear,
And all the winters are hidden.

ALFRED, LORD TENNYSON
Demeter and Other Poems, 1889

WEATHERS

This is the weather the cuckoo likes,
        And so do I;
When showers betumble the chestnut spikes,
        And nestlings fly;
And the little brown nightingale bills his best,
And they sit outside the "Traveller's Rest,"
And maids come forth sprig-muslin dressed,
And citizens dream of the South and West.
        And so do I.

This is the weather the shepherd shuns,
        And so do I;
When beeches drip in browns and duns,
        And thresh, and ply;
And hill-hid tides throb, throe on throe,
And meadow rivulets overflow,
And drops on gate-bars hang in a row,
And rooks in families homeward go,
        And so do I.

THOMAS HARDY

Late Lyrics in *The Complete Poems, 1922 edition*

It's raining, it's pouring,
The old man is snoring;
He went to bed and bumped his head
And couldn't get up in the morning!

ANON

A SWARM OF BEES

A swarm of bees in May
Is worth a load of hay;
A swarm of bees in June
Is worth a silver spoon;
A swarm of bees in July
Is not worth a fly.

ANON

MONDAY'S CHILD

Monday's child is fair of face,
Tuesday's child is full of grace,
Wednesday's child is full of woe,
Thursday's child has far to go,
Friday's child is loving and giving,
Saturday's child works hard for its living,
And a child that's born on the Sabbath day
Is blithe and bonny and good and gay.

ANON

WRITTEN IN MARCH

The cock is crowing,
The stream is flowing,
The small birds twitter,
The lake doth glitter,
The green field sleeps in the sun;
The oldest and the youngest
Are at work with the strongest;
The cattle are grazing,
Their heads never raising;
There are forty feeding as one!

Like an army defeated
The snow hath retreated,
And now doth fare ill
On the top of the bare hill;
The ploughboy is whooping – anon – anon:
There's joy in the mountains;
There's life in the fountains;
Small clouds are sailing,
Blue sky prevailing;
The rain is over and gone!

WILLIAM WORDSWORTH

Poems of the Imagination, 1807

Red sky at night,
Shepherd's delight;
Red sky in the morning,
Shepherd's warning.

ANON

March winds and April showers
Bring forth May flowers.

ANON

Come the oak before the ash,
My lady's sure to wear her sash;
Come the ash before the oak,
My lady's sure to wear her cloak.

ANON

If bees stay at home,
The rain will soon come;
If bees fly away,
It'll be a fine day.

ANON

WEATHER

Whether the weather be fine,
Or whether the weather be not,
Whether the weather be cold,
Or whether the weather be hot,
We'll weather the weather
Whatever the weather,
Whether we like it or not!

ANON

THE FIRST TOOTH

Through the house what busy joy,
Just because the infant boy
Has a tiny tooth to show!
I have got a double row,
All as white, and all as small;
Yet no one cares for mine at all.
He can say but half a word,
Yet that single sound's preferred
To all the words that I can say
In the longest summer day.
He cannot walk, yet if he put
With mimic motion out his foot,
As if he thought he were advancing,
It's prized more than my best dancing.

CHARLES AND MARY LAMB

Poetry for Children, 1809

A CALENDAR

January brings the snow,
Makes our feet and fingers glow.

February brings the rain,
Thaws the frozen lake again.

March brings breezes, loud and shrill,
To stir the dancing daffodil.

April brings the primrose sweet,
Scatters daisies at our feet.

May brings flocks of pretty lambs
Skipping by their fleecy dams.

June brings tulips, lilies, roses,
Fills the children's hands with posies.

Hot July brings cooling showers,
Apricots and gillyflowers.

August brings the sheaves of corn,
Then the harvest home is borne.

Warm September brings the fruit;
Sportsmen then begin to shoot.

Fresh October brings the pheasant;
Then to gather nuts is pleasant.

Dull November brings the blast;
Then the leaves are whirling fast.

Chill December brings the sleet,
Blazing fire, and Christmas treat.

SARA COLERIDGE

Pretty Lessons in Verse for Good Children, 1834

THE CLASSROOM

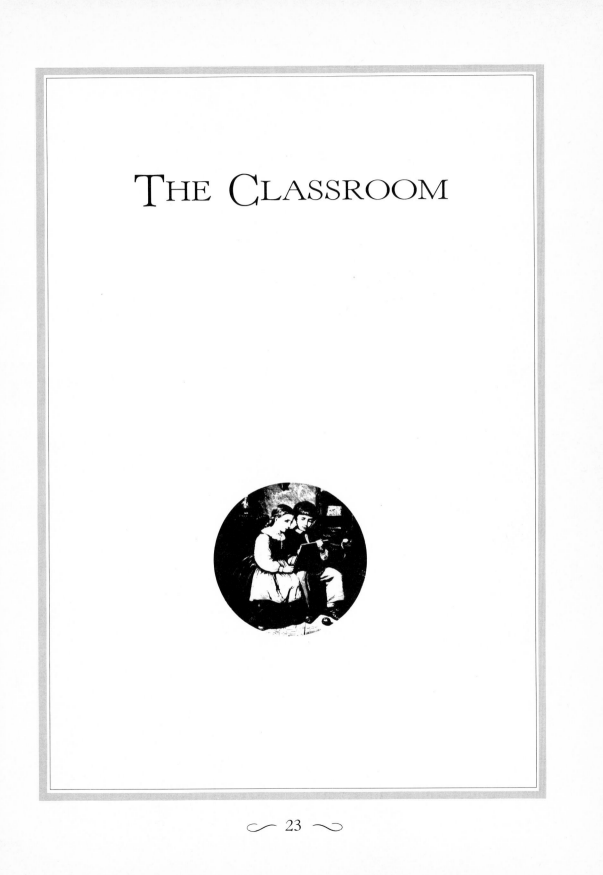

A was an Archer
who shot at a frog

B was a Butcher
who kept a bull-dog

C was a Captain
all covered with lace

D was a Drummer
who played with much grace

E was an Esquire
with pride on his brow

F was a Farmer
who followed the plough

G was a Gamester
who had but ill-luck

H was a Hunter
and hunted a buck

I was an Italian
who had a white mouse

J was a Joiner
and built up a house

K was a King
so mighty and grand

L was a Lady
who had a white hand

M was a Miser
who hoarded up gold

N was a Nobleman
gallant and bold

O was an Organ boy
who played about town

P was a Parson
who wore a black gown

Q was a Queen
who was fond of her people

R was a Robin
who perched on a steeple

S was a Sailor
who spent all he got

T was a Tinker
who mended a pot

U was an Usher
who loved little boys

V was a Veteran
who sold pretty toys

W was a Watchman
who guarded the door

X was eXpensive
and so became poor

Y was a Youth
who did not love school

Z was a Zany
who looked a great fool

ANON

THE OWL

There was an old owl who lived in an oak;
The more he heard, the less he spoke.
The less he spoke, the more he heard.
Why aren't we like that wise old bird?

ANON

DR. FOSTER

Doctor Foster is a good man,
He teaches children all he can:
Reading, writing, arithmetic,
And doesn't forget to use his stick.
When he does he makes them dance
Out of England into France,
Out of France into Spain,
Round the world and back again.

ANON

NATURAL HISTORY

What are little boys made of?
What are little boys made of?
Frogs and snails and puppy-dogs' tails,
And that are little boys made of.

What are little girls made of?
What are little girls made of?
Sugar and spice and all that's nice,
And that are little girls made of.

What are young men made of?
What are young men made of?
Sighs and leers, and crocodile tears,
And that are young men made of.

What are young women made of?
What are young women made of?
Ribbons and laces, and sweet pretty faces,
And that are young women made of.

ANON

JACK

That's Jack;
Lay a stick on his back!
What's he done? I cannot say.
We'll find out tomorrow,
And beat him today.

CHARLES HENRY ROSS

Ye Comical Rhymes of Ancient Times,
Dug up into Jokes for Small Folks, 1862

GOOD AND BAD CHILDREN

Children, you are very little,
And your bones are very brittle;
If you would grow great and stately,
You must try to walk sedately.

You must still be bright and quiet,
And content with simple diet;
And remain, through all bewild'ring,
Innocent and honest children.

Happy hearts and happy faces,
Happy play in grassy places –
That was how, in ancient ages,
Children grew to kings and sages.

But the unkind and unruly,
And the sort who eat unduly,
They must never hope for glory –
Theirs is quite a different story!

Cruel children, crying babies,
All grow up as geese and gabies,
Hated, as their age increases,
By their nephews and their nieces.

ROBERT LOUIS STEVENSON,
A Child's Garden of Verses, 1885

COMPARATIVES

Good, better, best,
Never let it rest,
Till your good is better
And your better best.

ANON

A DILLER, A DOLLAR...

A diller, a dollar,
A ten o'clock scholar;
What makes you come so soon?
You used to come at ten o'clock,
But now you come at noon!

ANON

ARITHMETIC

Multiplication is vexation,
Division is as bad;
The Rule of Three it puzzles me,
And fractions drive me mad.

ANON

THREE CHILDREN

Three children sliding on the ice,
All on a summer's day,
And it fell out, they all fell in,
The rest they ran away!

Now, had these children been at home,
Or sliding on dry ground,
Ten thousand pounds to a penny,
They had not all been drowned.

You parents all that children have,
And you that have got none,
If you would have them safe abroad,
Pray keep them safe at home.

TRADITIONAL

HOW TO WRITE A LETTER

Maria intended a letter to write,
But could not begin (as she thought) to indite;
So she went to her mother with pencil and slate,
Containing "Dear Sister," and also a date.

"With nothing to say, my dear girl, do not think
Of wasting your time over paper and ink;
But certainly this is an excellent way,
To try with your slate to find something to say.

"I will give you a rule," said her mother, "my dear,
Just think for a moment your sister is here,
And what would you tell her? Consider, and then
Though silent your tongue, you can speak with your pen."

ELIZABETH TURNER

The Crocus, 1844

TREES

The Oak is called the king of trees,
The Aspen quivers in the breeze,
The Poplar grows up straight and tall,
The Peach tree spreads along the wall,
The Sycamore gives pleasant shade,
The Willow droops in watery glade,
The Fir tree useful timber gives,
The Beech amid the forest lives.

SARA COLERIDGE

Pretty Lessons in Verse for Good Children, 1834

THE STORY OF FIDGETY PHILIP

"Let me see if Philip can
Be a little gentleman;
Let me see if he is able
To sit still for once at table":
Thus Papa bade Phil behave;
And Mama looked very grave.
But fidgety Phil,
He won't sit still;
He wriggles,
And giggles,
And then, I declare,
Swings backwards and forwards,
And tilts up his chair,
Just like any rocking-horse –
"Philip! I am getting cross!"

See the naughty, restless child
Growing still more rude and wild,
Till his chair falls over quite.
Philip screams with all his might,
Catches at the cloth, but then
That makes matters worse again.
Down upon the ground they fall,
Glasses, plates, knives, forks and all.
How Mama did fret and frown,
When she saw them tumbling down!
And Papa made such a face!
Philip is in sad disgrace.

Where is Philip, where is he?
Fairly covered up you see!
Cloth and all are lying on him;
He has pulled down all upon him.
What a terrible to-do!
Dishes, glasses, snapped in two!
Here a knife, and there a fork!
Philip, this is cruel work.
Table all so bare, and ah!
Poor Papa, and poor Mama
Look quite cross, and wonder how
They shall have their dinner now.

HEINRICH HOFFMANN

The English Struwwelpeter
(translator unknown), 1848

LITTLE THINGS

Little drops of water,
  Little grains of sand,
Make the mighty ocean
  And the beauteous land.

And the little moments,
  Humble though they be,
Make the mighty ages
  Of eternity.

So our little errors
   Lead the soul away,
From the paths of virtue
   Into sin to stray.

Little deeds of kindness,
   Little words of love,
Make our earth an Eden,
   Like the heaven above.

JULIA A. CARNEY

Hymns and Sacred Songs, 1855

HISTORY

Willy, Willy, Harry Stee,
Harry, Dick, John, Harry three,
One, two, three, Neds, Richard two,
Henry four, five, six, then who?
Edward four, five, Dick the bad,
Harrys twain and Ned the lad,
Mary, Bessy, James the vain,
Charlie, Charlie, James again!
William and Mary, Ann Gloria,
Four Georges, William – and Victoria!

ANON

THE MONTHS

Thirty days hath September,
April, June and November.
All the rest have thirty-one,
Excepting February alone,
Which has four and twenty-four
Till leap-year gives it one day more.

ANON

HERE LIES FRED

Here lies Fred,
Who was alive and is dead.
Had it been his father,
I had much rather;
Had it been his brother,
Still better than another;
Had it been his sister,
No one would have miss'd her;
Had it been the whole generation,
Still better for the nation;
But since 'tis only Fred,
Who was alive and is dead,
There's no more to be said.

ANON

LOOKING FORWARD

When I am grown to a man's estate
I shall be very proud and great,
And tell the other girls and boys
Not to meddle with my toys.

ROBERT LOUIS STEVENSON

A Child's Garden of Verses, 1885

Victor Gilbert

PLAYTIME

GIRLS AND BOYS COME OUT TO PLAY

Girls and boys, come out to play,
The moon doth shine as bright as day,
Leave your supper and leave your sleep,
And come with your playfellows into the street.
Come with a whoop or come with a call,
Come with a goodwill or not at all.
Up the ladder and down the wall,
A halfpenny roll will serve us all.
You find milk and I'll find flour,
And we'll have a pudding in half an hour!

ANON

One, two, buckle my shoe,
Three, four, shut the door,
Five, six, pick up sticks,
Seven, eight, lay them straight,
Nine, ten, a good fat hen,
Eleven, twelve, who will delve?
Thirteen, fourteen, maids a-courting,
Fifteen, sixteen, maids a-kissing,
Seventeen, eighteen, maids a-waiting,
Nineteen, twenty, my stomach's empty.

ANON

Rub-a-dub-dub,
Three men in a tub,
And how do you think they got there?
The butcher, the baker,
The candlestick-maker,
They all jumped out of a rotten potato,
T'was enough to make a man stare.

ANON

DON'T CARE

Don't-Care – he didn't care,
   Don't-Care was wild:
Don't-Care stole plum and pear
   Like any beggar's child.

Don't-Care was made to care,
   Don't-Care was hung:
Don't-Care was put in a pot
   And stewed till he was done.

ANON

ONE, TWO, THREE, FOUR, FIVE!

One, two, three, four, five!
"Once I caught a fish alive!"
Six, seven, eight, nine, ten!
"Then I let it go again."
"Why did you let it go?"
"Because it bit my finger so."
"Which finger did it bite?"
"This little finger on my right!"

ANON

A GOOD PLAY

We built a ship upon the stair
All made of the back-bedroom chairs,
And filled it full of sofa pillows
To go a-sailing on the billows.

We took a saw and several nails,
And water in the nursery pails;
And Tom said, "Let us also take
An apple and a slice of cake" –
Which was enough for Tom and me
To go a-sailing on, till tea.

We sailed along for days and days,
And had the very best of plays;
But Tom fell out and hurt his knee,
So there was no one left but me.

ROBERT LOUIS STEVENSON

A Child's Garden of Verses, 1885

ST. PAUL'S STEEPLE

Upon Paul's steeple stands a tree,
As full of apples as may be;
The little boys of London town,
They run with hooks to pull them down;
And then they run from hedge to hedge
Until they come to London Bridge.

ANON

Oranges and lemons, say the bells of St. Clement's;
You owe me five farthings, say the bells of St. Martin's;
When will you pay me, say the bells of Old Bailey;
When I grow rich, say the bells of Shoreditch;
When will that be? say the bells of Stepney;
I do not know, says the great bell of Bow.
Here comes a candle to light you to bed,
And here comes a chopper to chop off your head.

ANON

Ride a cock-horse to Banbury Cross,
To see a fine lady upon a white horse;
Rings on her fingers and bells on her toes,
And she shall have music wherever she goes.

ANON

See-saw, Margery Daw,
Johnny shall have a new master;
He shall have but a penny a day,
Because he can't work any faster.

ANON

Cock a doodle doo!
My dame has lost her shoe;
My master's lost his fiddling stick,
And don't know what to do.

Cock a doodle doo!
What is my dame to do?
Till master finds his fiddling stick,
She'll dance without her shoe.

Cock a doodle doo!
My dame has found her shoe,
And master's found his fiddling stick,
Sing doodle doodle doo!

Cock a doodle doo!
My dame will dance with you,
While master fiddles his fiddling stick
For dame and doodle doo.

ANON

TOM, JILL AND BOB

Tom tied a kettle to the tail of a cat,
Jill put a stone in the blind man's hat,
Bob threw his grandmother down the stairs –
And they all grew up ugly, and nobody cares.

ANON

As I was going to sell my eggs,
I met a man with bandy legs,
Bandy legs and crooked toes;
I tripped up his heels, and he fell on his nose.

ANON

As I was walking down the lake,
I met a little rattlesnake,
I gave him so much jelly-cake
It made his little belly ache.
One, two, three, out goes she!

ANON

AGAINST IDLENESS

My mother said
That I never should
Play with the gypsies
In the wood;
If I did she would say,
Naughty girl to disobey.
Your hair shan't curl,
Your shoes shan't shine,
You naughty girl
You shan't be mine.
My father said
That if I did
He'd bang my head
With the teapot lid.

The wood was dark,
The grass was green,
Up comes Sally
With a tambourine;
Alpaca frock,
New scarf-shawl,
White straw bonnet
And a pink parasol.
I went to the river –
No ship to get across,
I paid ten shillings
For an old blind horse;
I up on his back
And off in a crack,
Sally tell my mother
I shall never come back.

ANON

THE MULBERRY BUSH

Here we go round the mulberry bush,
        the mulberry bush,
        the mulberry bush,
Here we go round the mulberry bush,
All on a frosty morning.

This is the way we clap our hands,
This is the way we clap our hands,
This is the way we clap our hands,
All on a frosty morning.

ANON

You, North must go,
To a hut of snow
You, South in a trice,
To an island of spice;
You, off to China,
And sit on a hill!
And you to that chair,
And be five minutes still!

ANON

Ring-a-ring o'roses,
A pocket full of posies,
   A-tishoo! A-tishoo!
We all fall down.

The cows are in the meadow
Lying fast asleep,
   A-tishoo! A-tishoo!
We all get up again.

ANON

WHAT A TO-DO

What a to-do to die today
At a minute or two to two.
A thing distinctly hard to say,
But harder still to do.
For they beat a tattoo at twenty to two
Arrattatatatatatatatatoo
And the dragon will come
When he hears the drum
At a minute or two to two today
At a minute or two to two.

ANON

SUNNY DAYS

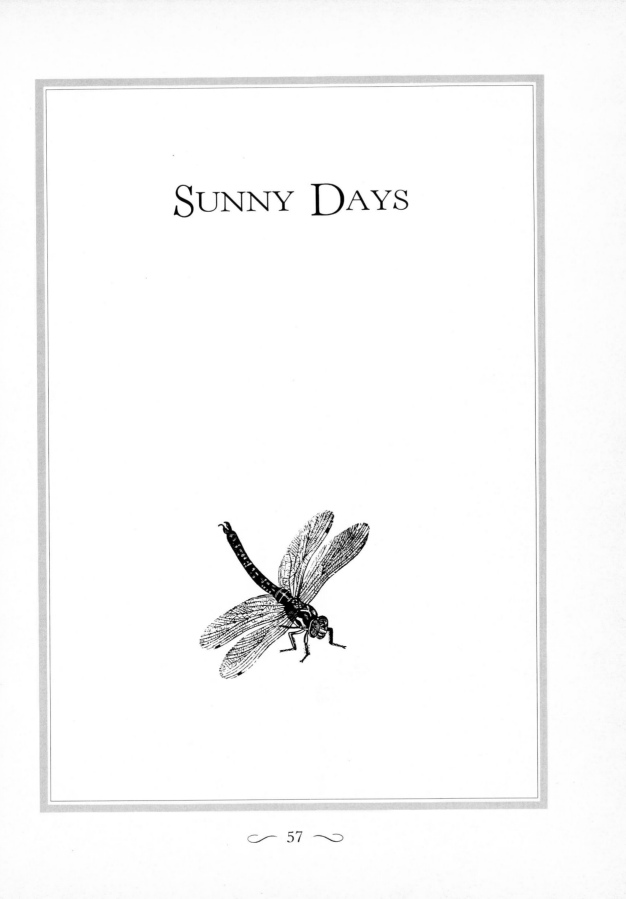

THE SKYLARK

The earth was green, the sky was blue:
　I saw and heard one sunny morn
A skylark hang between the two,
　A singing speck above the corn;

A stage below, in gay accord,
　White butterflies danced on the wing,
And still the singing skylark soared,
　And silent sank, and soared to sing.

The cornfield stretched a tender green
　To right and left beside my walks;
I knew he had a nest unseen
　Somewhere among the million stalks.

And as I paused to hear his song,
　While swift the sunny moments slid,
Perhaps his mate sat listening long,
　And listened longer than I did.

CHRISTINA GEORGINA ROSSETTI

Sing-Song, 1872

TUMBLING

In jumping and tumbling
    We spend the whole day,
Till night by arriving
    Has finished our play.

What then? One and all,
    There's no more to be said,
As we tumbled all day,
    So we tumble to bed.

ANON

I REMEMBER, I REMEMBER

I remember, I remember
The house where I was born,
The little window where the sun
Came peeping in at morn;
He never came a wink too soon
Nor brought too long a day;
But now, I often wish the night
Had borne my breath away.

I remember, I remember
The roses, red and white,
The violets and the lily-cups –
Those flowers made of light!
The lilacs where the robin built,
And where my brother set
The laburnum on his birthday, –
The tree is living yet!

I remember, I remember
Where I was used to swing,
And thought the air must rush as fresh
To swallows on the wing;
My spirit flew in feathers then
That is so heavy now,
The summer pools could hardly cool
The fever on my brow.

I remember, I remember
The fir-trees dark and high;
I used to think their slender tops
Were close against the sky:
It was a childish ignorance,
But now 'tis little joy
To know I'm farther off from Heaven
Than when I was a boy.

THOMAS HOOD

The Plea of the Midsummer Fairies, 1827

THE SWALLOW

Fly away, fly away, over the sea,
Sun-loving swallow, for summer is done.
Come again, come again, come back to me,
Bringing the summer and bringing the sun.

CHRISTINA GEORGINA ROSSETTI
Sing-Song, 1872

Sukey, you shall be my wife,
And I will tell you why:
I have got a little pig,
And you have got a sty;
I have got a dun cow,
And you can make good cheese;
Sukey, will you have me?
Say "yes," if you please.

ANON

A PROPOSAL

Bonny lass, pretty lass, wilt thou be mine?
Thou shalt not wash dishes,
Nor yet serve the swine;
Thou shalt sit on a cushion and sew a fine seam,
And thou shalt eat strawberries, sugar and cream!

TRADITIONAL

WHAT IS PINK?

What is pink? A rose is pink
By the fountain's brink.
What is red? A poppy's red
In its barley bed.
What is blue? The sky is blue
Where the clouds float through.
What is white? A swan is white
Sailing in the light.
What is yellow? Pears are yellow,
Rich and ripe and mellow.

What is green? The grass is green,
With small flowers between.
What is violet? Clouds are violet
In the summer twilight.
What is orange? Why, an orange,
Just an orange!

CHRISTINA GEORGINA ROSSETTI

Sing-Song, 1872

PIRATE STORY

Three of us afloat in the meadow by the swing,
  Three of us aboard in the basket on the lea.
Winds are in the air, they are blowing in the spring;
  And waves are on the meadow like the waves there are at sea.

Where shall we adventure, to-day that we're afloat.
  Wary of the weather and steering by a star?
Shall it be to Africa, a-steering of the boat,
  To Providence, or Babylon, or off to Malabar?

Hi! but here's a squadron a-rowing on the sea –
  Cattle on the meadow a-charging with a roar!
Quick, and we'll escape them, they're as mad as they can be,
  The wicket is the harbour and the garden is the shore.

ROBERT LOUIS STEVENSON
A Child's Garden of Verses, 1885

THE RIVER'S SONG

Clear and cool, clear and cool,
By laughing shallow, and dreaming pool;
Cool and clear, cool and clear,
By shining shingle, and foaming weir;
Under the crag where the ouzel sings,
And the ivied wall where the church-bell rings,
Undefiled, for the undefiled;
Play by me, bathe in me, mother and child.

Dank and foul, dank and foul,
By the smoky town in its murky cowl;
Foul and dank, foul and dank,
By wharf and sewer and slimy bank;
Darker and darker the further I go,
Baser and baser the richer I grow;
Who dare sport with the sin-defiled?
Shrink from me, turn from me, mother and child.

Strong and free, strong and free,
The floodgates are open, away to the sea.
Free and strong, free and strong,
Cleansing my streams as I hurry along,
To the golden sands, and the leaping bar,
And the taintless tide that awaits me afar,
As I lose myself in the infinite main,
Like a soul that has sinned and is pardoned again.
Undefiled, for the undefiled;
Play by me, bathe in me, mother and child.

CHARLES KINGSLEY

The Water Babies, 1863

THE RAINBOW

Boats sail on the rivers,
    And ships sail on the seas;
But clouds that sail across the sky
    Are prettier far than these.

There are bridges on the rivers,
    As pretty as you please;
But the bow that bridges heaven,
    And overtops the trees,
And builds a road from earth to sky,
    Is prettier far than these.

CHRISTINA GEORGINA ROSSETTI

Sing-Song, 1872

BED IN SUMMER

In winter I get up at night
And dress by yellow candle-light.
In summer quite the other way,
I have to go to bed by day.

I have to go to bed and see
The birds still hopping on the tree,
Or hear the grown-up people's feet
Still going past me in the street.

And does it not seem hard to you,
When all the sky is clear and blue,
And I should like so much to play,
To have to go to bed by day?

ROBERT LOUIS STEVENSON

A Child's Garden of Verses, 1885

DOWN IN YONDER MEADOW

Down in yonder meadow where the green grass
grows,
Pretty Pollie Pillicote bleaches her clothes.
She sang, she sang, she sang, oh, so sweet,
She sang, *Oh, come over!* across the street.

He kissed her, he kissed her, he bought her a gown,
A gown of rich cramoisie out of the town.
He bought her a gown and a guinea gold ring,
A guinea, a guinea, a guinea gold ring.

Up street, and down, shine the windows made of glass,
Oh, isn't Pollie Pillicote a braw young lass?
Cherries in her cheeks and ringlets in her hair,
Hear her singing *Handy Dandy* up and down the stair.

ANON

Lavender's blue, dilly, dilly,
Lavender's green.
When I am king, dilly, dilly,
You shall be queen.
Who told you so, dilly, dilly,
Who told you so?
'Twas mine own heart, dilly, dilly
That told me so.

Call up your men, dilly, dilly,
Set them to work,
Some with a rake, dilly, dilly,
Some with a fork.
Some to make hay, dilly, dilly,
Some to thresh corn,
Whilst you and I, dilly, dilly,
Keep ourselves warm.

ANON

IF NO ONE EVER MARRIES ME

If no one ever marries me –
And I don't see why they should,
For nurse says I'm not pretty,
And I'm seldom very good –

If no one ever marries me
I shan't mind very much,
I shall buy a squirrel in a cage
And a little rabbit-hutch;

I shall have a cottage near a wood,
And a pony all my own
And a little lamb, quite clean and tame,
That I can take to town.

And when I'm getting really old –
At twenty-eight or nine –
I shall buy a little orphan-girl
And bring her up as mine.

LAURENCE ALMA-TADEMA

Realm of Unknown Kings, 1897

THE CITY CHILD

Dainty little maiden, whither would you wander?
Whither from this pretty home, the home where mother dwells?
"Far and far away," said the dainty little maiden,
"All among the gardens, aurioulas, anemones,
Roses and lilies and Canterbury-bells."

Dainty little maiden, whither would you wander?
Whither from this pretty house, this city-house of ours?
"Far and far away," said the dainty little maiden,
"All among the meadows, the clover and the clematis,
Daisies and kingcups and honeysuckle flowers."

ALFRED, LORD TENNYSON

Sea Dreams and Idylls, 1860

THE MERMAID

Who would be
A mermaid fair,
Singing alone,
Combing her hair
Under the sea,
In a golden curl
With a comb of pearl,
On a throne?

I would be a mermaid fair;
I would sing to myself the whole of the day.
With a comb of pearl I would comb my hair;
And still as I combed I would sing and say,
"Who is it loves me? who loves not me?"
I would comb my hair till my ringlets would fall,
     Low adown, low adown,
And I should look like a fountain of gold
     Singing alone
     With a shrill inner sound,
     Over the throne
     In the midst of the hall.

ALFRED, LORD TENNYSON

Poems Chiefly Lyrical, 1830

CATKIN

I have a littly pussy
And her coat is silver-grey;
She lives in a great wide meadow
And she never runs away.
She'll always be a pussy,
She'll never be a cat,
Because – she's a pussy willow!
Now what do you think of that?

ANON

The man in the wilderness asked of me,
How many strawberries grow in the sea?
I answered him as I thought good,
As many red herrings as grow in the wood.

ANON

Mirror, mirror, tell me,
Am I pretty or plain?
Or am I downright ugly
And ugly to remain?
Shall I marry a gentleman?
Shall I marry a clown?
Or shall I marry old Knives and Scissors
A-shouting through the town?

ANON

ALL CREATURES GREAT AND SMALL

A LITTLE COCK SPARROW

A little cock sparrow sat on a tree,
Looking as happy as happy could be,
Till a boy came by with his bow and arrow:
Says, he, "I will shoot the little cock sparrow.

"His body will make me a nice little stew,
And perhaps there'll be some for a little pie too."
Says the little cock sparrow, "I'll be shot if I stay,"
So he flapped his wings and flew away.

ANON

FOUR-AND-TWENTY TAILORS

Four-and-twenty tailors went to kill a snail,
The best man among them durst not touch her tail;
She put out her horns like a little Kyloe cow:
Run, tailors, run! or she'll kill you all e'en now.

ANON

THE OWL

When cats run home and light is come
And dew is cold upon the ground,
And the far-off stream is dumb,
And the whirring sail goes round,
And the whirring sail goes round;
Alone and warming in his five wits,
The white owl in the belfry sits.

When merry milkmaids click the latch,
And rarely smells the new-mown hay,
And the cock hath sung beneath the thatch
Twice or thrice his roundelay,
Twice or thrice his roundelay;
Alone and warming his five wits,
The white owl in the belfry sits.

ALFRED, LORD TENNYSON

THE MOUSE AND THE CAKE

A mouse found a beautiful piece of plum cake,
The richest and sweetest that mortal could make;
'Twas heavy with citron and fragrant with spice,
And covered with sugar all sparkling as ice.

"My stars!" cried the mouse, while his eye beamed with glee,
"Here's a treasure I've found: what a feast it will be;
But, hark! there's a noise, 'tis my brothers at play;
So I'll hide with the cake, lest they wander this way.

"Not a bit shall they have, for I know I can eat
Every morsel myself, and I'll have such a treat."
So off went the mouse as he held the cake fast;
While his hungry young brothers went scampering past.

He nibbled, and nibbled, and panted, but still
He kept gulping it down till he made himself ill;
Yet he swallowed it all, and 'tis easy to guess,
He was soon so unwell that he groaned with distress.

His family heard him, and as he grew worse,
They sent for the doctor, who made him rehearse
How he'd eaten the cake to the very last crumb,
Without giving his playmates and relatives some.

"Ah me!" cried the doctor, "advice is too late;
You must die before long, so prepare for your fate.
If you had but divided the cake with your brothers,
'Twould have done you no harm, and been good for the others.

"Had you shared it, the treat had been wholesome enough;
But eaten by *one*, it was dangerous stuff;
So prepare for the worst –" and the word had scarce fled,
When the doctor turned round, the patient was dead.

Now all little people the lesson may take,
And *some* large ones may learn from the mouse and the cake;
Not to be over-selfish with what we may gain,
Or the best of our pleasures may turn into pain.

ELIZA COOK

Eliza Cook's Journal, 1849

CHOOSING THEIR NAMES

Our old cat has kittens three –
What do you think their names should be?

One is tabby with emerald eyes,
And a tail that's long and slender,
And into a temper she quickly flies
   If you ever by chance offend her.
      I think we shall call her this –
      I think we shall call her that –
Now, don't you think that *Pepperpot*
      Is a nice name for a cat?

One is black with a frill of white,
   And her feet are all white fur,
If you stroke her she carries her tail upright
   And quickly begins to purr.
      I think we shall call him this –
      I think we shall call him that –
Now, don't you think that *Sootikin*
      Is a nice name for a cat?

One is a tortoiseshell, yellow and black,
   With plenty of white about him;
If you tease him, at once he sets up his back,
   He's a quarrelsome one, ne'er doubt him.
      I think we shall call her this –
      I think we shall call her that –
Now, don't you think that *Scratchaway*
      Is a nice name for a cat?

Our old cat has kittens three
And I fancy these their names will be:
Pepperpot, Sootikin, Scratchaway – there!
Were ever kittens with these to compare?
And we call the old mother –
      Now what do you think? –
Tabitha Longclaws Tiddley Wink.

THOMAS HOOD

*A Garland of Verses for
Little People, 1866*

ALL THINGS BRIGHT
AND BEAUTIFUL

All things bright and beautiful,
　　All creatures great and small,
All things wise and wonderful,
　　The Lord God made them all.

Each little flower that opens,
　　Each little bird that sings,
He made their glowing colours,
　　He made their tiny wings.

The purple-headed mountain,
　　The river running by,
The sunset, and the morning,
　　That brightens up the sky;

The cold wind in the winter,
　　The pleasant summer sun,
The ripe fruits in the garden,
　　He made them every one.

He gave us eyes to see them,
　　And lips that we might tell,
How great is God Almighty,
　　Who has made all things well.

CECIL FRANCES ALEXANDER
Hymns for Little Children, 1848

DONKEY RIDING

Were you ever in Quebec,
Stowing timbers on a deck,
Where there's a king in his golden crown
Riding on a donkey?

Hey ho, and away we go,
Donkey riding, donkey riding,
Hey ho, and away we go,
Riding on a donkey.

Were you ever in Cardiff Bay,
Where the folks all shout, Hooray!
Here comes John with his three months' pay,
Riding on a donkey?

Hey ho, and away we go,
Donkey riding, donkey riding,
Hey ho, and away we go,
Riding on a donkey.

Were you ever off Cape Horn,
Where it's always fine and warm?
See the lion and the unicorn
Riding on a donkey.

Hey ho, and away we go,
Donkey riding, donkey riding,
Hey ho, and away we go,
Riding on a donkey.

ANON

THE DONKEY

When fishes flew and forests walked
　　And figs grew upon thorn,
Some moment when the moon was blood,
　　Then surely I was born;

With monstrous head and sickening cry
　　And ears like errant wings,
The devil's walking parody
　　On all four-footed things.

The tattered outlaw of the earth,
　　Of ancient crooked will;
Starve, scourge, deride me: I am dumb,
　　I keep my secret still.

Fools! For I also had my hour;
　　One far fierce hour and sweet:
There was a shout about my ears,
　　And palms before my feet!

G. K. CHESTERTON

The Wild Knight, 1900

THE ROBINS

A robin and a robin's son
Once went to town to buy a bun.
They couldn't decide on plum or plain,
And so they went back home again.

ANON

Little Robin Red-breast
Sat upon a rail,
Needle, naddle, went his head,
Wiggle, waggle, went his tail.

ANON

TO A BUTTERFLY

I've watched you now a full half-hour,
Self-poised upon that yellow flower;
And, little butterfly! indeed
I know not if you sleep or feed.
How motionless! Not frozen seas
More motionless! And then
What joy awaits you, when the breeze
Has found you out among the trees,
And calls you forth again!

This plot of orchard-ground is ours;
My trees they are, my sister's flowers;
Here rest your wings when they are weary,
Here lodge as in a sanctuary!
Come often to us, fear no wrong;
Sit near us on the bough!
We'll talk of sunshine and of song,
And summer days, when we are young;
Sweet childish days, that were as long
As twenty days are now.

WILLIAM WORDSWORTH

Poems Founded on the Affections, 1807

TWO LITTLE KITTENS

Two little kittens, one stormy night,
Began to quarrel, and then to fight;
One had a mouse, the other had none,
And that's the way the quarrel begun.

"I'll have that mouse," said the biggest cat;
"You'll have that mouse? We'll see about that!"
"I *will* have that mouse," said the eldest son;
"You *shan't* have the mouse," said the little one.

I told you before 'twas a stormy night
When these two little kittens began to fight;
The old woman seized her sweeping broom,
And swept the two kittens right out of the room.

The ground was covered with frost and snow,
And the two little kittens had nowhere to go;
So they laid them down on the mat at the door,
While the old woman finished sweeping the floor.

Then they crept in, as quiet as mice,
All wet with the snow, and as cold as ice,
For they found it was better, that stormy night,
To lie down and sleep than to quarrel and fight.

ANON

Pussy can sit by the fire and sing,
Pussy can climb a tree,
Or play with a silly old cork and string
to 'muse herself, not me.
But I like Binkie my dog, because
He knows how to behave;
So, Binkie's the same as the first Friend was,
And I am the Man in the Cave.

Pussy will play Man-Friday till
It's time to wet her paw
And make her walk on the window-sill
(For the footprint Crusoe saw);
Then she fluffles her tail and mews,
And scratches and won't attend.
But Binkie will play whenever I choose,
And he is my true first friend.

Pussy will rub my knees with her head
Pretending she loves me hard;
But the very minute I go to bed
Pussy runs out in the yard,
And there she stays till the morning-light;
So I know it is only pretend;
But Binkie, he snores at my feet all night,
and he is my Firstest Friend!

RUDYARD KIPLING

Just So Stories, 1902

I had a little pony
His name was Dapple-grey
I lent him to a lady
To ride a mile away
She whipped him
She slashed him
She rode him through the mire
I'll never let my pony now
For any lady's hire.

ANON

THE COUNTRY MOUSE AND THE CITY MOUSE

In a snug little cot lived a fat little mouse,
Who enjoyed, unmolested, the range of the house;
With plain food content, she would breakfast on cheese,
She dined upon bacon, and supped on grey peas.

A friend from the town to the cottage did stray,
And he said he was come a short visit to pay;
So the mouse spread her table as gay as you please,
And brought the nice bacon and charming grey peas.

The visitor frowned, and he thought to be witty:
Cried he, "You must know, I am come from the city,
Where we all should be shocked at provisions like these,
For we never eat bacon and horrid grey peas.

"To town come with me, I will give you a treat:
Some excellent food, most delightful to eat.
With me shall you feast just as long as you please;
Come, leave this fat bacon and shocking grey peas."

This kind invitation she could not refuse,
And the city mouse wished not a moment to lose;
Reluctant she quitted the fields and the trees,
The delicious fat bacon and charming grey peas.

They slyly crept under a gay parlour door,
Where a feast had been given the evening before;
And it must be confessed they on dainties did seize,
Far better than bacon, or even grey peas.

Here were custard and trifle, and cheesecakes good store,
Nice sweetmeats and jellies, and twenty things more;
All that art had invented the palate to please,
Except some fat bacon and smoking grey peas.

They were nicely regaling, when into the room
Came the dog and the cat, and the maid with a broom:
They jumped in a custard both up to their knees;
The country·mouse sighed for her bacon and peas.

Cried she to her friend, "Get me safely away,
I can venture no longer in London to stay;
For if oft you receive interruptions like these,
Give me my nice bacon and charming grey peas.

"Your living is splendid and gay, to be sure,
But the dread of disturbance you ever endure;
I taste true delight in contentment and ease,
And I *feast* on fat bacon and charming grey peas."

RICHARD SCRAFTON SHARPE

Old Friends in a New Dress, 1807

THE BIRD'S NEST

I'd not despoil the linnet's nest
    That whistles on the spray;
I'd not despoil the tuneful lark
    That sings at break of day;
I would not rob the charming thrush
    That chants so sweet at e'en;
Nor would not rob the lovely wren,
    With her bower of green.

The birds – they are like children
    That dance upon the lea;
And they will not sing in cages
    As they do in bush or tree.
They are just like tiny children
    Dear to their mother's heart;
And such as would the treasures steal
    Enact a cruel part!

ANON

Wire, briar, limber-lock,
Three geese in a flock;
One flew east, one flew west,
And one flew over the cuckoo's nest.

ANON

THE THREE LITTLE PIGS

A jolly old sow once lived in a sty,
　　And three little piggies had she,
And she waddled about saying "Umph! Umph! Umph!"
　　While the little ones said "Wee! wee!"

"My dear little brothers," said one of the brats,
　　"My dear little piggies," said he;
"Let us all for the future say, Umph! Umph! Umph!"
　　And they *wouldn't* say "Wee! wee! wee!"

So after a time these little pigs died,
　　They all died of *felo de se;**
From trying too hard to say "Umph! Umph! Umph!"
　　For they only could say "Wee! wee!"

MORAL
A moral there is to this little song,
　　A moral that's easy to see;
Don't try when you're young to say "Umph! Umph! Umph!"
　　For you only can say "Wee! wee!"

ALFRED SCOTT GATTY

Aunt Judy's Magazine, February 1870

*felo de se, self-murder

TEN LITTLE MICE

Ten little mice sat in a barn to spin,
Pussy came by, and popped her head in:
What are you at, my jolly ten?
We're making coats for gentlemen.
Shall I come in and cut your threads?
No, Miss Puss, you'd bite off our heads.

ANON

DING DONG BELL

Ding dong bell! Pussy's in the well!
Who put her in? Little Tommy Lin.
Who pulled her out? Little Tommy Stout.
What a naughty boy was that
To drown poor pussy-cat,
Who ne'er did any harm,
But killed all the mice in father's barn.

TRADITIONAL

BIRDS OF A FEATHER

Birds of a feather flock together
And so do pigs and swine,
Rats and mice will have their choice,
And so will I have mine.

ANON

PUSSY

I like little pussy, her coat is so warm;
And if I don't hurt her, she'll do me no harm.
So I'll not pull her tail, nor drive her away,
But pussy and I very gently will play.
She shall sit by my side, and I'll give her some food;
And she'll love me because I am gentle and good.

I'll pat pretty pussy, and then she will purr;
And thus show her thanks for my kindness to her.
But I'll not pinch her ears, nor tread on her paw,
Lest I should provoke her to use her sharp claw.
I never will vex her, nor make her displeased –
For pussy don't like to be worried and teased.

ANON

THE SPIDER AND THE FLY

"Will you walk into my parlour?" said the Spider to the Fly,
"'Tis the prettiest little parlour that ever you did spy;
The way into my parlour is up a winding stair,
And I have many curious things to show when you are there."
"Oh no, no," said the little Fly, "to ask me is in vain,
For who goes up your winding stair can ne'er come down again."

"I'm sure you must be weary, dear, with soaring up so high;
Will you rest upon my little bed?" said the Spider to the Fly.
"There are pretty curtains drawn around, the sheets are fine and thin;
And if you like to rest awhile, I'll snugly tuck you in!"
"Oh no, no," said the little Fly, "for I've often heard it said,
They never, never wake up again, who sleep upon your bed!"

Said the cunning Spider to the Fly, "Dear friend, what can I do,
To prove the warm affection I've always felt for you?
I have within my pantry good store of all that's nice;
I'm sure you're very welcome – will you please to take a slice?"
"Oh no, no," said the little Fly, "kind sir, that cannot be,
I've heard what's in your pantry, and I do not wish to see."

"Sweet creature," said the Spider, "you're witty and you're wise;
How handsome are your gauzy wings, how brilliant are your eyes!
I have a little looking-glass upon my parlour shelf,
If you'll step in a moment, dear, you shall behold yourself."
"I thank you, gentle sir," she said, "for what you're pleased to say,
And bidding you good morning now, I'll call another day."

The Spider turned him round about, and went into his den,
For well he knew the silly Fly would soon come back again;
So he wove a subtle web, in a little corner sly,
And set his table ready, to dine upon the Fly.
Then he came out to his door again, and merrily did sing:
"Come hither, hither, pretty Fly, with the pearl and silver wing;
Your robes are green and purple – there's a crest upon your head;
Your eyes are like the diamond bright, but mine are dull as lead."

Alas, alas! how very soon this silly little Fly,
Hearing his wily, flattering words, came slowly flitting by;
With buzzing wings she hung aloft, then near and nearer drew,
Thinking only of her brilliant eyes, and green and purple hue;
Thinking only of her crested head – poor foolish thing! At last,
Up jumped the cunning Spider, and fiercely held her fast.
He dragged her up his winding stair, into his dismal den,
Within his little parlour – but she ne'er came out again!

MARY HOWITT
The New Year's Gift, 1829

SOME OLD FRIENDS

YOUNG AND OLD

When all the world is young, lad,
   And all the trees are green;
And every goose a swan, lad,
   And every lass a queen;
Then hey for boot and horse, lad,
   And round the world away;
Young blood must have its course, lad,
   And every dog his day.

When all the world is old, lad,
   And all the trees are brown;
When all the sport is stale, lad,
   And all the wheels run down;
Creep home, and take your place there,
   The spent and maimed among:
God grant you find one face there,
   You loved when all was young.

CHARLES KINGSLEY
The Water Babies, 1863

THE GINGERBREAD MAN

Smiling girls, rosy boys,
Come and buy my little toys;
Monkeys made of gingerbread,
And sugar horses painted red.

ANON

Sam, Sam, the butcher man,
Washed his face in a frying pan,
Combed his hair with a wagon wheel,
And died with a toothache in his heel.

ANON

Doctor Foster went to Gloucester
In a shower of rain;
He stepped in a puddle,
Right up to his middle,
And never went there again.

ANON

WINIFRED WATERS

Winifred Waters sat and sighed
   Under a weeping willow;
When she went to bed she cried,
   Wetting all her pillow;

Kept on crying night and day,
   Till her friends lost patience;
"What shall we do to stop her, pray?"
   So said her relations.

Send her to the sandy plains
   In the zone called torrid.
Send her where it never rains,
   Where the heat is horrid.

Mind that she has only flour
   For her daily feeding;
Let her have a page an hour
   Of the driest reading –

Navigation, logarithm,
   All that kind of knowledge –
Ancient pedigrees go with 'em
   From the Herald's College.

When the poor girl has endured
   Six months of this drying,
Winifred will come back cured,
   Let us hope, of crying.

WILLIAM BRIGHTY RANDS

Lilliput Lyrics, 1899

THERE WAS AN OLD WOMAN

There was an old woman tossed up in a basket
Nineteen times as high as the moon;
Where she was going I couldn't but ask it,
For in her hand she carried a broom.

"Old woman, old woman, old woman," quoth I,
"Oh whither, Oh whither, Oh whither, so high?"
"To brush the cobwebs off the sky!"
"Shall I go with thee?" "Ay, by-and by."

ANON

THE OLD WOMAN OF NORWICH

There was an old woman, and what do you think?
She lived upon nothing but victuals and drink;
Victuals and drink were the chief of her diet —
Yet this plaguey old woman could never be quiet!

TRADITIONAL

COBBLER, COBBLER

Cobbler, cobbler, mend my shoe,
Get it done by half past two;
Stitch it up, and stitch it down,
Then I'll give you half a crown.

ANON

The lion and the unicorn
Were fighting for the crown;
The lion beat the unicorn
All round the town.
Some gave them white bread,
And some gave them brown;
Some gave them plum cake,
And sent them out of town.

ANON

JEMIMA

There was a little girl, and she had a little curl,
Right in the middle of her forehead,
And when she was good, she was very, very good,
But when she was bad she was horrid.

One day she went upstairs while her parents, unawares,
In the kitchen down below were at their meals,
And she stood upon her head, on her little truckle bed,
And she then began hurraying with her heels.

Her mother heard the noise, and thought it was the boys,
A-playing at a combat in the attic,
But when she climbed the stair and saw Jemima there,
She took her and did spank her most emphatic!

ANON

MARY, MARY...

Mary, Mary, quite contrary,
How does your garden grow?
With silver bells, and cockle-shells,
And pretty maids all in a row.

TRADITIONAL

I am Queen Anne, of whom 'tis said
I'm chiefly famed for being dead,
Queen Anne, Queen Anne, she sits in the sun,
As fair as a lily, as brown as a bun.

ANON

THE QUEEN OF HEARTS

The Queen of Hearts,
She made some tarts,
All on a summer's day,
The Knave of Hearts,
He stole the tarts,
And took them clean away.

The King of Hearts
Called for the tarts
And beat the Knave full sore.
The Knave of Hearts
Brought back the tarts,
And vowed he'd steal no more.

ANON

THE JOLLY MILLER

There was a jolly miller once
Lived on the river Dee;
He worked and sang from morn till night,
No lark more blithe than he.
And this the burden of his song
Forever used to be,
"I care for nobody, no, not I,
And nobody cares for me!"

TRADITIONAL

THE DAUGHTER OF THE FARRIER

The daughter of the farrier
Could find no one to marry her,
Because she said
She would not wed
A man who could not carry her.

The foolish girl was wrong enough,
And had to wait quite long enough;
For as she sat
She grew so fat
That nobody was strong enough.

ANON

MY PRETTY PINK

My pretty little pink, I once did think
That you and I would marry,
But now I've lost all hopes of that,
I can no longer tarry.

I've got my knapsack on my back,
My musket on my shoulder,
To march away to Quebec Town,
To be a gallant soldier.

Where coffee grows on a white-oak-tree,
And the rivers flow with brandy,
Where the boys are like a lump of gold,
And the girls as sweet as candy.

ANON

THE LITTLE MAN AND MAID

There was a little man
And he woo'd a little maid,
And he said, "Little maid, will you wed, wed, wed?
I have little more to say
Than 'will you, yea or nay?'
For least said is soonest mended-ded-ded-ded."

The little maid replied,
(Some say a little sighed,)
"But what shall we have to eat, eat eat?
Will the love that you are rich in
Make a fire in the kitchen?
Or the little god of loving turn the spit, spit spit?"

TRADITIONAL

JOSHUA LANE

"I know I have lost my train,"
Said a man named Joshua Lane;
"But I'll run on the rails
With my coat-tails for sails
And maybe I'll catch it again."

ANON

I had a little nut-tree,
Nothing would it bear
But a silver nutmeg
And a golden pear;
The King of Spain's daughter
She came to visit me,
And all for the sake of my little nut-tree.
I skipped over water,
I danced over sea,
And all the birds in the air couldn't catch me.

ANON

Sing a song of sixpence,
A pocket full of rye;
Four and twenty blackbirds
Baked in a pie!

When the pie was opened
The birds began to sing;
Was not that a dainty dish
To set before the king?

The king was in his counting-house
Counting out his money;
The queen was in the parlour,
Eating bread and honey.

The maid was in the garden,
Hanging out the clothes;
When down came a blackbird
And snapped off her nose.

ANON

SWEET DREAMS

WYNKEN, BLYNKEN AND NOD

Wynken, Blynken and Nod one night
Sailed off in a wooden shoe –
Sailed on a river of crystal light,
Into a sea of dew.
"Where are you going and what do you wish?"
The old moon asked the three.
"We have come to fish for the herring-fish
That live in this beautiful sea;
Nets of silver and gold have we,"
Said Wynken, Blynken, and Nod.

The old moon laughed and sang a song,
As they rocked in the wooden shoe,
And the wind that sped them all night long
Ruffled the waves of dew.
The little stars were the herring-fish
That lived in that beautiful sea –
"Now cast your nets wherever you wish –
But never afeared are we";
So cried the stars to the fishermen three:
Wynken, Blynken and Nod.

All night long their nets they threw
To the stars in the twinkling foam –
Then down from the skies came the wooden shoe,
Bringing the fishermen home;
'Twas all so pretty a sail, it seemed
As if it could not be,
And some folks thought 'twas a dream they'd dreamed
Of sailing the beautiful sea –
But I shall name you the fishermen three:
Wynken, Blynken, and Nod.

Wynken and Blynken are two little eyes,
And Nod is a little head,
And the wooden shoe that sailed the skies
Is a wee one's trundle-bed.
So shut your eyes while mother sings
Of wonderful sights that be,
And you shall see the beautiful things
As you rock on the misty sea,
Where the old shoe rocked the fishermen three:
Wynken, Blynken, and Nod.

EUGENE FIELD

A Little Book of Western Verse, 1889

WINTER TIME

Late lies the wintry sun a-bed,
A frosty, fiery sleepy-head;
Blinks but an hour or two; and then,
A blood-red orange, sets again.

Before the stars have left the skies,
At morning in the dark I rise;
And shivering in my nakedness,
By the cold candle, bathe and dress.

Close by the jolly fire I sit
To warm my frozen bones a bit;
Or with a reindeer-sled, explore
The colder countries round the door.

When to go out, my nurse doth wrap
Me in my comforter and cap,
The cold wind burns my face, and blows
Its frosty pepper up my nose.

Black are my steps on silver sod;
Thick blows my frosty breath abroad;
And tree and house, and hill and lake,
Are frosted like a wedding cake.

ROBERT LOUIS STEVENSON
A Child's Garden of Verses, 1885

WINDY NIGHTS

Whenever the moon and stars are set,
   Whenever the wind is high,
All night long in the dark and wet,
   A man goes riding by.
Late in the night when the fires are out,
Why does he gallop and gallop about?

Whenever the trees are crying aloud,
   And ships are tossed at sea,
By, on the highway, low and loud,
   By at the gallop goes he.
By at the gallop he goes, and then
By he comes back at the gallop again.

ROBERT LOUIS STEVENSON
A Child's Garden of Verses, 1885

NOW THE DAY IS OVER

Now the day is over,
 Night is drawing nigh,
Shadows of the evening
 Steal across the sky.

Now the darkness gathers,
 Stars begin to peep,
Birds and beasts and flowers
 Soon will be asleep.

Jesu, give the weary
 Calm and sweet repose;
With thy tenderest blessing
 May our eyelids close.

Grant to little children
 Visions bright of thee;
Guard the sailors tossing
 On the deep blue sea.

Comfort every sufferer
  Watching late in pain;
Those who plan some evil
  From their sin restrain.

Through the long night-watches
  May thine angels spread
Their white wings above me,
  Watching round my bed.

When the morning wakens,
  Then may I arise
Pure and fresh and sinless
  In thy holy eyes.

Glory to the Father,
  Glory to the Son,
And to thee, blest Spirit,
  Whilst all ages run.

SABINE BARING-GOULD
Hymns Ancient and Modern, 1868

THE CELESTIAL SURGEON

If I have faltered more or less
In my great task of happiness;
If I have moved among my race
And shown no shining morning face;
If beams from happy human eyes
Have moved me not; if morning skies,
Books, and my food, and summer rain
Knocked on my sullen heart in vain:
Lord, thy most pointed pleasure take
And stab my spirit broad awake.

ROBERT LOUIS STEVENSON

Underwoods, 1887

CERTAINTY

I never saw a moor,
I never saw the sea;
Yet know I how the heather looks,
And what a wave must be.

I never spoke with God,
Nor visited in heaven;
Yet certain am I of the spot
As if the chart were given.

EMILY DICKINSON

The Poems, 1855

WHERE DID YOU COME FROM, BABY DEAR?

Where did you come from, baby dear?
Out of the everywhere into here.

Where did you get your eyes so blue?
Out of the sky as I came through.

What makes the light in them sparkle and spin?
Some of the starry spikes left in.

Where did you get that little tear?
I found it waiting when I got here.

What makes your forehead so smooth and high?
A soft hand stroked it as I went by.

What makes your cheek like a warm white rose?
I saw something better than anyone knows.

Whence that three-cornered smile of bliss?
Three angels gave me at once a kiss.

Where did you get this pearly ear?
God spoke, and it came out to hear.

Where did you get those arms and hands?
Love made itself into hooks and bands.

Feet, whence did you come, darling things?
From the same box as the cherubs' wings.

How did they all just come to be you?
God thought about me, and so I grew.

But how did you come to us, you dear?
God thought about you, and so I am here.

GEORGE MACDONALD

At the Back of the North Wind, 1871

THE SNOW

It sifts from leaden sieves,
It powders all the wood,
It fills with alabaster wool
The wrinkles of the road.

It makes an even face
Of mountain and of plain,
Unbroken forehead from the east
Unto the east again.

It reaches to the fence,
It wraps it, rail by rail,
Till it is lost in fleeces;
It flings a crystal veil

On stump and stack and stem,
The summer's empty room,
Acres of seams where harvests were,
Recordless, but for them.

It ruffles wrists of posts,
As ankles of a queen,
Then stills its artisans like ghosts,
Denying they have been.

EMILY DICKINSON

The Poems, 1855

Matthew, Mark, Luke and John,
Bless the bed that I lie on.
If I should die before I wake,
I pray the Lord my soul to take.

ANON

"How many miles is it to Babylon?"
"Three score miles and ten."
"Can I get there by candle-light?"
"Yes, and back again!
If your heels are nimble and light,
You may get there by candle-light."

ANON

A CHRISTMAS CAROL

In the bleak mid-winter
    Frosty wind made moan,
Earth stood hard as iron,
    Water like a stone;
Snow had fallen, snow on snow,
    Snow on snow,
In the bleak mid-winter
    Long ago.

Our God, heaven cannot hold Him,
    Nor earth sustain;
Heaven and Earth shall flee away
    When He comes to reign:
In the bleak mid-winter
    A stable-place sufficed
The Lord God Almighty
    Jesus Christ.

What can I give Him,
    Poor as I am?
If I were a shepherd
    I would bring a lamb;
If I were a wise man
    I would do my part –
Yet what I can, I give Him,
    Give my heart.

CHRISTINA GEORGINA ROSSETTI

Sing-Song, 1872

AN EVENING SCENE

The sheep-bell tolleth curfew time;
    The gnats, a busy rout,
Fleck the warm air; the dismal owl
    Shouteth a sleepy shout;
The voiceless bat, more felt than seen,
    Is flitting round about.

The aspen leaflets scarcely stir;
    The river seems to think;
Athwart the dusk, broad primroses
    Look coldly from the brink,
Where, listening to the freshet's noise,
    The quiet cattle drink.

The bees boom past; the white moths rise
    Like spirits from the ground;
The gray flies hum their weary tune,
    A distant, dream-like sound;
And far, far off, to the slumb'rous eve,
    Bayeth an old guard-hound.

COVENTRY PATMORE

Poems, 1906

THE STAR

Twinkle, twinkle, little star,
How I wonder what you are!
Up above the world so high,
Like a diamond in the sky.

When the blazing sun is gone,
When he nothing shines upon,
Then you show your little light,
Twinkle, twinkle, all the night.

Then the traveller in the dark,
Thanks you for your tiny spark,
He could not see which way to go,
If you did not twinkle so.

In the dark blue sky you keep,
And often through my curtains peep,
For you never shut your eye,
Till the sun is in the sky.

As your bright and tiny spark,
Lights the traveller in the dark –
Though I know not what you are,
Twinkle, twinkle, little star.

JANE TAYLOR

Rhymes for the Nursery, 1806

STAR LIGHT, STAR BRIGHT...

Star light, star bright,
First star I've seen tonight,
Wish I may, wish I might,
Have this wish I wish tonight.

ANON

I see the moon, and the moon sees me.
God bless the moon, and God bless me.

ANON

EVENING

The day is past, the sun is set,
　And the white stars are in the sky;
While the long grass with dew is wet,
　And through the air the bats now fly.

The lambs have now lain down to sleep,
　The birds have long since sought their nests;
The air is still; and dark, and deep
　On the hill side the old wood rests.

Yet of the dark I have no fear,
　But feel as safe as when 'tis light;
For I know God is with me there,
　And He will guard me through the night.

For God is by me when I pray,
　And when I close mine eyes in sleep,
I know that He will with me stay,
　And will all night watch by me keep.

For He who rules the stars and sea,
　Who makes the grass and trees to grow,
Will look on a poor child like me,
　When on my knees I to Him bow.

He holds all things in His right hand,
　The rich, the poor, the great, the small;
When we sleep, or sit, or stand,
　Is with us, for He loves us all.

THOMAS MILLER

Original Poems for My Children, 1850

THE LAND OF NOD

From breakfast on through all the day
At home among my friends I stay,
But every night I go abroad
Afar into the land of Nod.

All by myself I have to go,
With none to tell me what to do –
All alone beside the streams
And up the mountainside of dreams.

The strangest things are there for me,
Both things to eat and things to see,
And many frightening sights abroad
Till morning in the land of Nod.

Try as I like to find the way,
I never can get back by day,
Nor can remember plain and clear
The curious music that I hear.

ROBERT LOUIS STEVENSON

A Child's Garden of Verses, 1885

THE LAND OF STORY-BOOKS

At evening when the lamp is lit,
Around the fire my parents sit;
They sit at home and talk and sing,
And do not play at anything.

Now, with my little gun I crawl
All in the dark along the wall,
And follow round the forest track
Away behind the sofa back.

There, in the night, where none can spy,
All in my hunter's camp I lie,
And play at books that I have read
Till it is time to go to bed.

These are the hills, these are the woods,
These are my starry solitudes;
And there the river by whose brink
The roaring lions come to drink.

I see the others far away.
As if in firelit camp they lay,
And I, like to an Indian scout,
Around their party prowled about.

So, when my nurse comes in for me,
Home I return across the sea,
And go to bed with backward looks
At my dear land of Story-Books.

ROBERT LOUIS STEVENSON

A Child's Garden of Verses, 1885

ROCK-A-BYE BABY...

Rock-a-bye baby,
On the treetop;
When the wind blows,
The cradle will rock;
When the bough breaks,
The cradle will fall;
Down will come cradle,
Baby and all!

TRADITIONAL

ALL THROUGH THE NIGHT

Sleep, my babe, lie still and slumber,
All through the night;
Guardian angels God will lend thee,
All through the night;
Soft and drowsy hours are creeping,
Hill and vale in slumber sleeping,
Mother dear her watch is keeping,
All through the night.

God is here, thou'lt not be lonely,
All through the night;
'Tis not I who guards thee only,
All through the night.
Night's dark shades will soon be over,
Still my watchful care shall hover,
God with me His watch is keeping,
All through the night.

ANON

THE POETS

ALEXANDER, Cecil Frances
(1818–1895) Ireland
Born in Co. Wicklow, Ireland. In 1850 she
married the Rev. William Alexander, who
was to become Archbishop of Armagh.
Hymns for Little Children (1848) includes not
only "All Things Bright and Beautiful" but
also "Once in Royal David's City" and "There
is a Green Hill Far Away."

ALMA-TADEMA, Laurence
(1865–1940) UK
Daughter of the pre-Raphaelite painter Sir
Lawrence Alma-Tadema. A close friend of
the pianist and politician Paderewski. She
died a spinster, as she had prophesied.

BARING-GOULD, Sabine (1834–1924)
UK
Author of "Onward Christian Soldiers" and
159 published works, including novels, travel
books, histories and collections of folk songs.
A rich man by birth, he worked as a curate
and vicar in the churches and mission schools
of Yorkshire in England before returning to
take up living on his family estates in Devon.

CARNEY, Julia A. (1823–1908) USA
A schoolteacher from Boston. It is said that
she improvised "Little Things" as an edifying
tract while teaching class one day in 1845.

CHESTERTON, Gilbert Keith
(1874–1936) UK
Poet, novelist, critic and artist, Chesterton
was extraordinarily prolific. Among his works
are full-length studies of Dickens, Browning,
Stevenson, and St. Thomas Aquinas. He is
principally famous, however, for the Father
Brown stories. A stubborn and formidable
battler with his pen, Chesterton was
renowned in real life for his bumbling
absent-mindedness and his unfailing ability
to get lost.

COLERIDGE, Sara (1802–1852) UK
The daughter of Samuel Taylor Coleridge.
Brought up in the company of Southey and
Wordsworth near Keswick in England's Lake
District, in 1829 she married her cousin
Henry Coleridge and moved to London.
Aside from *Pretty Lessons in Verse for Good*
Children (1834), and a fairy story,
Phantasmion (1837), she produced no original
work, but devoted herself to editing and
annotating her father's works. It is widely
believed that she thus denied the world one
of its most sensitive and intelligent poets.

COOK, Eliza (1818–1889) UK
Eliza Cook started to compose verse before
she was fifteen. Her first published book
appeared in 1835, when she was just
seventeen. She contributed verses to many
London journals – at first anonymously and
then, after the immense success of a poem
called "The Old Arm Chair," openly and
profitably. Eventually, in 1849, she started
her own publication, *Eliza Cook's Journal*.
The last issue was printed in 1854. Her
greatest contribution to literature was that
she drew attention to the forgotten talents of
Thomas Hood (q.v.). Eliza Cook lived in
London throughout her life.

DICKINSON, Emily Elizabeth
(1830–1886) USA
The daughter of a wealthy lawyer from
Amherst, Massachusetts, Emily Dickinson
lived the quiet life of a respectable,
intellectual spinster. She had several very
intelligent male friends, but was otherwise a
recluse for the latter twenty-five years of her
life. No one knew until she died that she had
written more than a thousand poems of
remarkable sensitivity and originality. Like
the English naturalist, Gilbert White, she
expressed the sharp, ecstatic pangs
occasioned by everyday things precisely
observed. Her images were eccentric, witty
and concise.

FIELD, Eugene (1850–1895) USA
Born in St. Louis, Missouri, Field was a
columnist with the *Chicago Morning News*,
contributing literary and humorous pieces or
light verse. "Wynken, Blynken and Nod" was
written in bed "upon brown wrapping paper"
one night in March 1889 when the entire
poem suddenly came into his head.

GATTY, Alfred Scott (1847–1918) UK
Gatty held the highest heraldic order –
Garter King of Arms (1904). He was also a

song writer and contributed verses to his mother's *Aunt Judy's Magazine*.

HARDY, Thomas (1840–1928) UK
Poet and novelist. Initially an architect, Hardy wrote a large number of very popular novels about his native Dorset, including *Tess of the d'Urbervilles* (1891) and *Jude the Obscure* (1895). He regarded fiction, however, merely as a means of making a living, and longed instead to write verse. After the publication of *Jude the Obscure* he gave up novel writing and devoted the rest of his life to poetry. Although they use conventional forms, Hardy's poems are startlingly original in tone and in syntax.

HOFFMANN, Heinrich (1809–1894) Germany
A Frankfurt doctor, Hoffmann worked in an asylum. He wrote and illustrated *Struwwelpeter* as a moral lesson book that would not frighten its readers.

HOOD, Thomas (1799–1845) UK
Born in London, the son of a Scottish bookseller and printer, Hood contributed to magazines and studied engraving before appointment as sub-editor on the *London Magazine*, where he met de Quincey, Lamb, and others. The great parodist John Hamilton Reynolds became Hood's closest friend and collaborator, and Hood married his sister. He edited several magazines and his works achieved considerable popularity, notably the *Song of the Shirt* (1843) and the *Bridge of Sighs* (1843), which combine the faint tone of pathos so characteristic of Hood's work and the jaunty humor which, according to his friends, he always evinced.

HOWITT, Mary (1799–1888) UK
Née Botham. Wife of author William Howitt and mother of twelve children, Mary Howitt, a Quaker, collaborated with her husband and published more than a hundred books in her own right. Among other claims to fame, she was the first English translator of Hans Christian Andersen.

KINGSLEY, Charles (1819–1875) UK
Born in England at Holne, Dartmoor, Kingsley became rector of Eversley in Hampshire (1844) after a Cambridge education. A novelist, journalist, and historian, he was Professor of Modern History at Cambridge from 1860 to 1869.

KIPLING, (Joseph) Rudyard (1865–1936) UK
Born in Bombay and educated in England, Kipling returned to India in 1882 and rapidly acquired a reputation as a brilliant reporter and satirical poet. He settled in London in 1889. His most popular works include *The Jungle Books* (1894–5), *Stalky and Co.* (1899), *Kim* (1901), and *Just So Stories* (1902). He was a fine wordsmith; "A word," he said, "should fall in its place like a bell in a full chime."

LAMB, Charles (1775–1834) and **Mary** (1764–1847) UK
Although a humorous and gentle man, Charles Lamb was haunted by fear of hereditary madness. His elder sister, Mary, murdered their mother in 1796, after which he took Mary into his care. His best known work is contained in the *Essays of Elia* (1823). Charles and Mary were coauthors of *Tales from Shakespeare* (1807), an attempt to render Shakespeare's plots accessible to children. Charles's famous poem "On an Infant Dying as Soon as Born" (1827), concerns the baby son of his friend and collaborator Thomas Hood (q.v.).

MACDONALD, George (1824–1905) UK
Scottish novelist and poet. Educated at Aberdeen University and at Highbury Congregationalist College where he became a pastor, he is best remembered for *At the Back of the North Wind* (1871), *The Princess and Curdie* (1882), and *The Princess and the Goblin* (1871). Macdonald had eleven children of his own.

MILLER, Thomas (1807–1874) UK
An illiterate English basket-weaver from Nottingham, Miller taught himself to read and write. He had his poems delivered to Lady Blessington in baskets he had made himself. Once she had expressed her approval the rest of London followed suit.

PATMORE, Coventry (1823–1896) UK
Amateur of chemistry, Coleridge scholar and Assistant Keeper of the British Library in London. His best known work, the intimate serial poem "The Angel in the House" (1862) is a celebration of every aspect of married life: Patmore was happily married three times. He restricted himself largely to traditional verse forms but longed to experiment, like Gerard Manley Hopkins (with whom he had a correspondence) with meter.

RANDS, William Brighty
(1823–1882) UK
A self-educated children's poet who was born and spent most of his life in or about West London.

ROSS, Charles Henry (1841–1897) UK
At first Ross was a clerk at the British Public Records Office at Somerset House in London, and then a cartoonist, editor of *Judy*, a rhymester, and author.

ROSSETTI, Christina Georgina
(1830–1894) UK
Sister of the poet and painter Dante Gabriel Rossetti, Christina led a sad life and failed to fulfill her early exceptional promise. She twice rejected suitors because of her high Anglican religious principles, and her verses are devout and full of the sadness of "what might have been." Her first collection, *Goblin Market* (1862), was very much her finest, but *Sing-Song* (1872) is full of charming, simple verses for children. She was always frail and, at the time of *Sing-Song's* composition, was very close to death from Grave's disease. Thereafter, she taught with her mother and wrote morally improving verse.

SHARPE, Richard Scrafton
(c.1775–1852) UK
A London grocer who wrote copious comic verse anonymously and only revealed his identity in 1837.

STEVENSON, Robert Louis
(1850–1894) UK
A master stylist and supremely imaginative writer who contrived to lead a hero's life despite often crippling illness. All his life he suffered from chronic bronchial problems and acute nervous excitability. Stevenson nonetheless traveled extensively, wrote many fine essays and novels and in *A Child's Garden of Verses* (1885) applied his highly developed gifts of imagination and sympathy to the emotions and enthusiasms of childhood. In so doing he can be said to have invented a whole new genre of verse. In 1888 he travelled in the South Seas and at last settled with his family in Samoa where the natives called him "Tusitala" (the tale-teller). He died there of a brain hemorrhage. His novels include *Treasure Island* (1883), *Kidnapped* (1886), *Catriona* (1893), and, for older readers, the eerie *Strange Case of Dr. Jekyll and Mr. Hyde* (1886).

TAYLOR, Jane (1783–1824) UK
With her sister Ann, Jane Taylor was the best known children's poet of her time. They lived together at their family home in Colchester, Essex.

TENNYSON, Alfred, Lord (1809–1892) UK
Although the most honored and fêted poet of the Victorian era, Tennyson liked to live "far from the madding crowd" in Hampshire or on the Isle of Wight. He was very prolific and, although he never wrote specifically for children, many of his works have become firm favorites with young people because of their grand romantic subject matter or because they are ideal for reciting.

TURNER, Elizabeth
(1775–1846) UK
A popular children's poet, Elizabeth Turner lived at Whitchurch in Shropshire. All her books had the names of flowers: "The Daisy" (1807), "The Cowslip" (1811), "The Pink" (1823), and "The Bluebell" (1838).

WORDSWORTH, William (1770–1850) UK
Poet Laureate. He lived at Grasmere in the English Lake District with his sister Dorothy. At his best, as in "The Prelude" or "Tintern Abbey," Wordsworth was a brilliant, thoughtful nature poet; at his worst he was capable of gaucheness and banality.

THE PAINTERS

A BRIEF NOTE ON SOME OF THE ANONYMOUS VERSES
The age of some familiar rhymes is consistently surprising. "I Had a Little Nut-tree ..." for example, refers to the visit of Joanna of Castile to the court of Henry VI in 1506. "Multiplication is Vexation" is first found in a manuscript of 1570. "Thirty Days hath September" is quoted in *Return From Parnassus*, a drama of 1606, while "Sing a Song of Sixpence" is quoted by Beaumont and Fletcher. "A Swarm of Bees in May" is, at the least, three hundred years old, as is "Ride a Cock-Horse" (Banbury Cross – one of the *"chere reine"* crosses – was demolished in the seventeenth century). "I had a little pony" has been found in various forms, including (c.1630): "I had a little bonny nagg/his name was Dapple Gray;/And he would bring me to an ale-house/A mile out of my way ..." An early variant of "Three Children Sliding on the Ice" dates back to 1662.

page

Title	Charles Sims (1873–1928)
6	Ernest Walbourn (fl.1897–1904)
10	Arthur Hacker (1858–1919)
14	Leopold Rivers (1850–1905)
15	Erskine Nicol (1825–1904)
19	Marie Firmin-Girard (1838–1921)
22	L.M. Watson (nineteenth century)
26	Johann Georg Meyer von Bremen (nineteenth century)
27	Ralph Hedley (1851–1913)
29	Harold H. Piffard (fl.1895–1899)
32	James Hayllar (1829–1920)
33	Edmund George Warren (1834–1909)
36	Joseph Farquharson (1847–1935)
40	Victor Gilbert (1847–1933)
45	Alexander M. Rossi (fl.1870–1903)
48	William Bromley (fl.1835–1888)
49	Giovanni Battista Torriglia (b.1858)
52	William Stewart MacGeorge (1861–1931)
56	James Valentine Jelley (fl.1885–1942)
60	Helen Allingham (1848–1926)
64	Basil Bradley (1842–1904)
65	Alfred Augustus Glendening (fl.1861–1903)
66	James Hayllar (1829–1920)
70	Percy Harland Fisher (b.1876)
71	Sir William MacTaggart (1835–1910)
74	James Hayllar (1829–1920)
75	William Stephen Coleman (1829–1904)
78	John Frederick Herring (fl.1860–1875)
83	Philip Eustace Stretton (fl.1884–1919)
86	Luigi Chialiva (nineteenth century)
91	Augusta Innes Withers (fl.1829–1865)
93	Albert Durer Lucas (1828–1918)
97	Edward Killingworth Johnson (1825–1923)
100	Charles Edward Wilson (fl.1891–1936)
101	Luigi Chialiva (nineteenth century)
104	Alexander Koester (1864–1932)
105	C. Blair (nineteenth century)
108	George Sheridan Knowles (1863–1931)
113	Alexander M. Rossi (fl.1870–1903)
116	Anon.
117	Helen Allingham (1848–1926)
120	E. Thomas Hale (fl. from 1898)
121	Frederick Goodall (1822–1904)
124	Henry Le Jeune (1819–1904)
127	Edward Robert Hughes (1851–1914)
130	Fred Hall (1860–1948)
134	Joseph Farquharson (1846–1935)
139	Edward Ridley (nineteenth century)
143	John Atkinson Grimshaw (1863–1893)
146	George Smith (1829–1901)
Endpapers	John Samuel Raven (1829–77)

INDEX OF FIRST LINES

A

A birdie with a yellow bill	8
A diller, a dollar,	30
A jolly old sow once lived in a sty,	102
A little cock sparrow sat on a tree,	80
All things bright and beautiful,	87
A mouse found a beautiful piece of plum cake,	82
A robin and a robin's son	90
As I was going to sell my eggs,	51
As I was walking down the lake,	51
A swarm of bees in May	14
At evening when the lamp is lit,	145
A was an archer	24

B

Birds of feather flock together	104
Boats sail on the rivers,	69
Bonnie lass, pretty lass, wilt thou be mine?	64

C

Children, you are very little,	28
Clear and cool, clear and cool,	68
Cobbler, cobbler, mend my shoe,	115
Cock a doodle doo!	50
Cock Robin got up early	9
Cocks crow in the morn	8
Come the oak before the ash,	17

D

Dainty little maiden, whither would you wander?	74
Ding dong bell! Pussy's in the well!	103
Doctor Foster is a good man,	25
Doctor Foster went to Gloucester	111
Donkey, donkey, old and gray,	9
Don't-Care – he didn't care	43
Down in yonder meadow where the green grass grows,	71

F

Fly away, fly away, over the sea,	62
Four-and-twenty tailors went to kill a snail,	80
From breakfast on through all the day	144

G

Get up, get up, you lazyhead,	9
Girls and boys, come out to play,	42
Good, better, best,	30

H

Here lies Fred,	39
Here we go round the mulberry bush,	54
"How many miles is it to Babylon?"	136

I

I am Queen Anne, of whom 'tis said	118
I'd not despoil the linnet's nest,	100
If bees stay at home,	17
If I have faltered more or less	132
If no one ever marries me –	73
I had a little nut-tree,	122
I had a little pony	96
I have a little pussy	76
"I know I have lost my train,"	122
I like little pussy, her coat is so warm;	105
In a snug little cot lived a fat little mouse,	98
I never saw a moor,	132
In jumping and tumbling	59
In the bleak mid-winter	137
In winter I get up at night	70
I remember, I remember	60
I see the moon and moon sees me.	141
It sifts from leaden sieves,	135
It's raining, it's pouring,	13
I've watched you now a full half-hour,	92

J

January brings the snow,	21

L

Late lies the wintry sun a-bed,	128
Lavender's blue, dilly, dilly,	72
"Let me see if Philip can	34
Little drops of water,	36
Little Robin Red-breast	90

M

March winds and April showers	17
Maria intended a letter to write,	32
Mary, Mary, quite contrary,	117
Matthew, Mark, Luke and John,	136
Mirror, mirror, tell me,	77
Monday's child is fair of face,	15

Multiplication is vexation, 30
My mother said 53
My pretty little pink, I once did think 120

N

Now the day is over, 130

O

One, two, buckle my shoe, 42
One, two, three, four, five! 44
Oranges and lemons, say the bells
  of St. Clement's; 47
Our old cat has kittens three — 84

P

Pussy can sit by the fire and sing, 95

R

Red sky at night, 17
Ride a cock-horse to Banbury Cross, 48
Ring-a-ring o'roses, 55
Rock-a-bye, baby, 146
Rub-a-dub-dub, 43

S

Sam, Sam, the butcher man, 111
See-saw, Margery Daw, 49
See the naughty, restless child 35
Sing a song of sixpence, 123
Sleep, my babe, lie still and slumber, 147
Smiling girls, rosy boys, 110
Star light, star bright, 141
Sukey, you shall be my wife, 63
"Summer is coming, summer is coming, 12

T

Ten little mice sat in a barn to spin, 103
That's Jack; 27
The cock is crowing, 16
The day is past, the sun is set, 142
The lion and the unicorn 115
The man in the wilderness asked of me, 76
The Oak is called the king of trees, 33
The Queen of Hearts 118
The sheep-bell tolleth curfew time; 138

The earth was green, the sky was blue; 58
The daughter of the farrier 119
There was a jolly miller once 119
There was a little girl, and she had
  a little curl, 116
There was a little man 121
There was an old owl who lived in an oak; 25
There was an old woman, and what
  do you think? 114
There was an old woman tossed up
  in a basket 114
Thirty days hath September, 38
This is the weather the cuckoo likes, 13
Three children sliding on the ice, 31
Three of us afloat in the meadow
  by the swing, 66
Tom tied a kettle to the tail of a cat, 51
Through the house what busy joy, 20
Twinkle, twinkle, little star, 140
Two little kittens, one stormy night, 94

U

Upon Paul's steeple stands a tree, 47

W

We built a ship upon the stair 46
Were you ever in Quebec, 88
What a to-do to die today 55
What are little boys made of? 26
When cats run home and light is come 81
What is pink? A rose is pink 65
When all the world is young, lad, 110
Whenever the moon and stars are set, 129
When fishes flew and forests walked 89
When I am grown to a man's estate 39
Where did you come from, baby dear? 133
Whether the weather be fine, 18
Who has seen the wind? 11
Who would be/A mermaid fair, 75
"Will you walk into my parlour?"
  said the Spider to the Fly, 106
Willy, Willy, Harry Stee, 38
Winifred Waters sat and sighed 112
Wire, briar, limber-lock 101
Wynken, Blynken and Nod one night 126

Y

You, North must go, 54